A Long-Ago Place

Donna Betten

To order additional copies of this book, contact:
Xlibris
1-888-795-4274
www.Xlibris.com
Orders@Xlibris.com

ISBN: Softcover   978-1-7960-6546-6
          EBook   978-1-7960-6545-9

Print information available on the last page

Rev. date: 10/10/2019

A Long-Ago Place

by
Donna Betten

Illustrated by

Julie Westmaas

Dedicated to mothers everywhere in the world
who once were little girls.

Long-Ago Place

The gentle *cooing of a pigeon always transports* my thoughts to a quiet place. Rays of sunshine dance on top of my arms and legs, tingling warmth into the middle of my soul. I squint one eye to look at the sky. Where is that sound coming from? I wish I could see what color the bird is. I shift as the trunk begins to jab sharp pieces of bark into my back. I rub the dancing rays of sunshine off my legs, but still I feel their footprints left burning on my skin.

I gently lean my head back on the tree while the cooing carries off into the distance. My closed eyes open to white puffs of clouds. They look so much like cotton candy that on a day like today, I wish to pull a cloud toward my mouth. *Hmm.* My mind imagines its sugary-sweet taste.

The sweet sound of another bird fills my ear. I don't know what it is or where it is coming from, but I hear it every day. I know it well. I know that sound, for every morning, I hear it from my bed. I know that sound as well as the sweet perfume scent of the gardenia bush. The perfume hangs heavy on the air. Everything is so still, so real. It is as though I am still sitting there as the bitter smell of the dying purple flowers try to rob me of the perfect afternoon far away and a long time ago.

This place is where I dreamed of the woman I would become and of the mother I would have to be to Porky, Jemoo, Serena, Lindy Loo, Semolina, Wendy, Suzanna, Pinky, and of course, the one-eyed teddy, Teddy. All the children sit waiting for the imaginary door to fly open and for their mother to come home from a busy ten minutes of being a secretary. The door opens, and each child gets a kiss for being so well-behaved and for not moving. This brief moment of affection is followed with a frantic burst of cleaning energy.

During my absence from home, a handful of plump, ripe, sweet deeply purple mulberries had fallen from the tree and stained my living room's dirt floor. So I get my fig twig broom and clean up the mess at once. With swift strokes, I cleaned my living room—only to notice that mulberries have landed on my stove! So I will have to sweep that rock off before I can give all the children their bath—on the same rock (as soon as it is not a stove anymore).

With all the cleaning done, the only thing left to do is face the chore of supper. What shall I make tonight? Perhaps mulberries might be a nice change. But that will mean the children will have to wait while Mama goes to the grocery store to gather the mulberries. Just let me get my purse, and I will be on my way. I give a goodbye kiss to everyone, and the door closes on a happy, quiet home under the mulberry tree—just the way it's supposed to be.

Well, supper is interrupted by the nagging thumb-to-nose screaming of an older sister to come in and take a bath. I load Porky, Jemoo, Serena, Lindy Lindy Loo, Semolina, Wendy, Suzanna, Pinky, and of course, Teddy in the baby carriage and push them back to the house.

The air is cool now. It, too, seems to be gently moving. And on its winds, the sweet smells of the gardenias and evening primroses softly caress my memory. The sky has turned into a canvas of pale shades of pink, purple, and gold. Its sunrays have stopped tap-dancing on my skin and seem to be floating into pirouettes with the clouds as their dance partners. The sound of plates clinking onto the table chimes the end of another perfect day.

Then somewhere far away, the cooing of a pigeon is heard again. Another bird joins in. I know it well, but I have never seen it, and I don't know what color it is. This is the place I remember well; this is the place far away that I like so well. But it seems like I visit this place less and less as the years go by. Sometimes the pigeon coos just as I wonder what to make for supper for my children, and I realize that one day long ago, I acted out today. It was perfect then and is perfect today.

Draw or write about your playhouse or fort.

Is it real or pretend?

Draw or write about your favorite game. Is it real or pretend?

Draw or write about yourself.

Printed in the United States
By Bookmasters